Contents

Some words are printed in bold, **like this**. You can find out what they mean by looking in the glossary on page 52.

It was a quiet night at the chemical factory in the sleepy town of Savenner.

And that was the gobal hit, "Rolling in the..."

Whoo-hoo

Suddenly there's an explosion.

Sirens wailing, firefighters arrive at the scene.

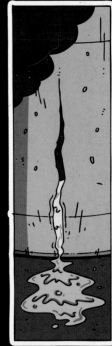

By the next morning, firefighters were starting to get the fire under control. But the fire was not the only threat to the town...

Early the next morning, as firefighters tackle the blaze, chemicals are still bubbling...

While the emergency crews make the plant safe and tend to the injured, investigators begin the task of working out what caused the explosion. The scene is a giant puzzle of wreckage. It contains clues and evidence that investigators will use to help them understand the chemical reactions and events involved in the disaster, so that they can untangle the story of what happened. And now a full investigation begins.

The investigation begins

Can you imagine having to deal with fire, choking smoke, and damage at a chemical factory? How would you go about working out what happened, and whether it was an accident or not? This book focuses on a fictional accident at a place called Savenner, but it is based on a real event that took place in Louisiana, USA, in 1995. It is all about what people do to sort out the mess after a serious chemical accident. It is also a book about **chemical reactions**.

What are chemical reactions?

A chemical reaction is a change that makes at least one new substance. For example, carbon and oxygen are two different substances. They react together to make a new substance – carbon dioxide. Some chemical reactions are dangerous. They cause fires, **explosions**, or the release of harmful substances.

Why investigate?

There are several reasons why people investigate this kind of accident. The first is to check to see if there is a continuing hazard. If dangerous chemical reactions are going on, could they cause further damage or injure more people?

The second reason is to find out exactly what happened, and to understand who or what was responsible. This is not just to blame someone or something for an accident. It is also to learn from mistakes and to prevent additional, similar accidents in the future.

Starting an investigation

It is important to sort out and investigate chemical accidents quickly. In most cases, people report accidents within minutes or hours after they happen. But sometimes people fail to report incidents, and then agencies cannot deal with the hazards caused by the accident or interview eyewitnesses while they recall events most clearly. In the United Kingdom, the Health and Safety Executive and the Environment Agency are responsible for dealing with chemical incidents and safety.

HOW IT WORKS

The steps in a chemical accident investigation are similar to the steps people take in a scientific experiment. In an experiment, scientists test a **hypothesis**, or idea, by trying to find evidence to support or disprove it. They then carefully record results and come to a conclusion based on them. Accident investigators work in a similar way, following these steps:

1   They form one or several hypotheses about how the accident might have happened.

2. They search for and carefully record evidence, or **data**, about what happened. For example, they may collect and analyse samples of substances found at the accident site or interview eyewitnesses about what they saw before and during the accident.

3. They study and consider the data. Based on these findings, investigators conclude which, if any, hypothesis is correct.

4. They make recommendations about how to prevent future, similar chemical accidents.

A firefighter talks to a specialist in dealing with **hazardous** materials. These are some of the specialists who take part in dealing with a dangerous chemical spill.

Who investigates?

As soon as the accident at the chemical factory is reported, an investigation team springs into action. The skills needed by team members are varied, but most use scientific, **engineering**, technological, and mathematical skills to do their work, some of which they first studied in school. For example, some of the team members use their medical knowledge to evaluate the health impact of the substances released in the accident. Others use their knowledge of forces to study the damage to buildings and equipment caused by explosions.

Teamwork

Investigators may work for many different organizations. Some work for government agencies that are responsible for ensuring public and environmental safety. Others may work for organizations representing the chemical industry and are responsible for making factories safer and less polluting. Some may work for specialized companies with expert knowledge of particular types of substances. With all of these people involved in an investigation team, it is essential to have a lead investigator to pull together different evidence.

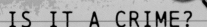

IS IT A CRIME?

Police forces get involved in investigating some chemical accidents. This sometimes happens when there is a possibility that a fire or other damage was caused intentionally as a criminal act. It also happens when there are suspicions that a chemical company did not have sufficient safety precautions in place, for example, to prevent injury to workers or damage to buildings and the environment.

FORENSIC SCENE INVESTIGATOR

A forensic scene investigator gathers evidence that may be used in a legal case to decide if a crime has been committed and who might be responsible.

Forensic scene investigators specialize in using a range of scientific techniques and equipment to find evidence at the scene of a murder, an accident site, or any other place where a crime may have been committed. They find and carefully collect evidence, which they pass on to detectives and to forensic laboratories for analysis. A forensic scene investigator will often have a university degree in a science such as chemistry or a specialized forensic science degree.

Forensic scene investigators usually work in teams. They cordon off the accident scene to keep people out partly because the scene might be dangerous. But also because people going in could disturb or obscure clues that may suggest the accident was not accidental. Here. Chinese police are guarding the entrance to a coal mine after a mining accident.

Chemical processes

After an accident at a chemical factory, investigators will want to know what substances are made or used there. Some useful substances are found naturally, such as sand, iron ore, and crude oil. These raw materials are used to make other useful substances – through chemical reactions – in factories. For example, glass, steel, and plastic are made from raw materials in chemical factories. Industries around the world make and use around 40,000 substances.

Iron is an important substance that we use to make everything from engines and cutlery to bridges and supertankers. People extract iron from iron ore rock. This is achieved by using a chemical reaction in incredibly hot blast furnaces such as the one shown here.

Reactions and changes

A chemical reaction happens to one or several substances called **reactants**. During the reaction, the reactants disappear, because they change into one or more new substances called **products**. For example, eggs, milk, and flour are reactants, and pancakes are products of a reaction that happens after we cook batter!

Most reactions are irreversible, meaning the product cannot be changed back into the reactants. For example, pancakes cannot be turned back into the individual ingredients that made them, because they have undergone a **chemical change**.

Chemical changes are different from **physical changes**. In physical changes, the original substances do not change chemically. For example, you can **dissolve** salt in water to make a salty solution. But you can separate the two again by heating to **evaporate** the water, leaving salt crystals chemically identical to the salt you dissolved.

IRON AND SULFUR

Iron filings are a grey powder, while sulfur is a yellow powder. When you mix them together at room temperature, there is no chemical reaction. You can separate the mixture using a magnet, because the iron is a magnetic material, but the sulfur is not. But when you heat the powders using a Bunsen burner, a chemical reaction happens between the two reactants. The product is a black powder. We can show the reaction as symbols:

iron + sulfur $\longrightarrow$ Chemical change $\longrightarrow$ iron sulfide
Fe + S caused by heat FeS

Chemical hazards

Some substances are highly dangerous. This is because of how they react with other substances – anything from air or water to substances that make up living things. Substances may be poisonous, cause injuries or illnesses, explode, or start fires.

WHAT IS GOING ON?

One of the first things the chemical accident investigation team does is find out what substances could be involved. Factories have detailed records of what substances they have stored, are making, or plan to make. Many factories have licences and permits that allow their workers to handle potentially hazardous materials.

The team members investigating the accident at the Savenner chemical factory think they have a problem at first: the office where the documents were stored burned down during the fire. Luckily, they manage to find copies stored elsewhere. They confirm that the factory had three storage tanks that stored turpentine. This is a **flammable** liquid that is used, for example, to make paint less sticky and to dissolve different substances. A guard who escaped from the site and several eyewitnesses are all convinced that the blast came from near the tanks of turpentine.

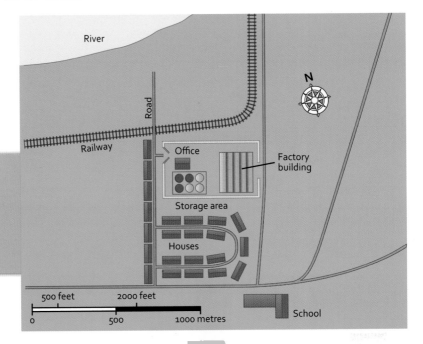

This is a map of the chemical factory at Savenner. You can see six storage tanks for substances. The three red ones contained turpentine.

In a chemical accident, a harmful substance may be released directly, or it may be created when several less harmful substances react together. Many countries have laws that require chemical factories to take great precautions when handling certain substances. However, producing, transporting, storing, and disposing of substances can all be hazardous. Unless hazards are controlled, there is the risk of an accident happening.

A survivor of the Bhopal gas tragedy demonstrates against Union Carbide, currently owned by Dow Chemicals. Protestors hope to bring those responsible for the accident to justice and for the thousands of affected survivors to be paid fairly for the years of suffering they have endured as a result of the accident.

Worst chemical accident of all time

In December 1984, factory workers at the Union Carbide chemical factory in Bhopal, India, were washing out pipes. What they did not know was that a valve in the pipes was faulty. As a result, water was dripping into a giant underground tank containing 38 tonnes of methyl isocyanate. Methyl isocyanate is a very dangerous substance that requires careful storage, because it reacts violently with water, releasing gases and heat. The reaction with the dripping water caused pipes from the tank to burst, releasing tonnes of methyl isocyanate gas over the city of Bhopal. The gas was so deadly that it killed nearly 10,000 people, and it injured or blinded over half a million people.

Site destruction

The accident at the Savenner chemical factory began with an explosion, but this was soon followed by a major fire. When investigators start their work, the fire is still blazing and is so incredibly hot that it is impossible for them to get near the blast site. What caused the fire, and why is it so difficult to put out? Let's start with **atoms**.

Atoms

All substances (and everything else in the world!) are made up of tiny pieces of matter called atoms. Atoms have a central part called a **nucleus**, and tiny particles called **electrons** circle around this. The electrons are pulled towards the nucleus by electrostatic forces. These are forces like those that hold a balloon to a wall after it has been rubbed against a jumper. A **molecule** is made up of several atoms held together, because electrons are shared by each nucleus. The forces between atoms are called **bonds**.

The burning reaction

Burning is one sort of chemical reaction. This reaction needs energy – usually from heat – to begin. The energy is needed to break bonds between atoms in the reactants, and also to make new ones between atoms in the product. Materials burn when their atoms make new bonds with oxygen atoms. That is why the burning reaction is sometimes called oxidation.

As we have seen, the investigative team suspects that turpentine played a role in the industrial accident. Turpentine is made from many carbon and hydrogen atoms. These react with oxygen to make carbon dioxide, carbon monoxide, and water.

Forest fires spread because air heated by one burning tree can start the burning reaction in the next, and so on.

Fuels such as wood store chemical energy that is released when the fuel burns.

Giving out heat

Some reactions use so much energy that they take heat from the surroundings. They are **endothermic**. Other reactions produce more energy than they need to make compounds, so they release energy as heat into their surroundings. They are **exothermic**. Burning is probably the most common exothermic reaction. The excess heat produced during burning drives the reaction faster and faster, until the reactants are used up.

Investigators know from records that there was enough turpentine on site to fill 16,000 baths! No wonder the fire burned for so long and got so hot.

CHEMICAL DATA TABLE
Turpentine

Physical state: Liquid

Odour: Distinctive

Flammable: Yes

Products of burning: Carbon oxides (CO, CO_2).

Firefighting

You probably know about the "fire triangle", which is a visual aid that summarizes the three factors that a fire needs to keep burning:

Air
A source of
oxygen

Heat
Enough to make the fuel
start to react and keep
on reacting

Fuel
Something that
will burn

The job of firefighters is to remove one or more of these factors so that the fire dies down and stops. With many fires, firefighters spray on water. Water evaporates from the heat of the fire, producing steam or water **vapour**. This takes up space that oxygen would occupy near the flame, so the fire cannot get the oxygen it needs. Evaporation uses up heat and therefore helps cool smoke, air, walls, and objects that are burning or getting hot enough to catch fire. Firefighters try to cut off the fuel supply, too, for example by closing valves on tanks, or by cutting gaps into a forest so that a fire cannot pass from tree to tree.

Foam liquid is pumped from a tank and gas is blown through it to make many bubbles. The foam then coats burning substances to block oxygen and slow the burning reaction.

Firefighters cannot use water to stop all fires. Burning fuels such as oil float on water and may spread the fire. Substances such as sodium metal react with water to release poisonous products. In such cases, firefighters **extinguish** fires using powders, foams, or carbon dioxide, to keep oxygen away from the fuel.

In the Savenner factory accident, the turpentine fire would normally have been put out using foam. However, the first firefighters to arrive had no access to foam, so they used water to cool the burning tanks and storage area until foam became available. Once the firefighters extinguish the fire, fire investigators can start their work.

Day 1, 11.30 p.m.
The first fire team arrives at the fire.

Day 2, 12.15 a.m.
The second fire team arrives, because the fire is too big for the first to control alone.

Fire investigators move into accident sites where fires have raged to look for clues as to how, why, or where the fire started. They need to be very careful, as they might encounter unsafe buildings and hazardous materials in places damaged by fire.

FIRE INVESTIGATOR

A fire investigator (sometimes called a fire scene investigator, or FSI) gathers evidence to determine the cause and origin of a fire.

Fire investigators use scientific knowledge of what buildings are made of and how fire affects those materials. They are experts on how fires behave and how burn patterns are left in fire-damaged sites. They search for evidence suggesting how fires started. The job involves some detective work, but many fire investigators often have a degree in engineering – for example, civil engineering, which is the study of the design and construction of anything from buildings to bridges.

Explosive reactions

Fire investigators know that the fire at the chemical factory followed an explosion. Explosions are an extreme form of exothermic reaction. An explosion releases lots of energy and usually produces large volumes of gas. Some of this energy creates high temperatures that heat the gas. Gas molecules spread out and move faster when they are heated. The hot gases from an explosion expand and push away the air around the reaction, sending out a **shock wave** through air. The vibration of air creates a loud bang.

A massive hotel in Shenyang, China, is demolished using the power of carefully planned detonations of explosives positioned throughout the building.

There are two main types of explosive reaction:

- **Deflagrations** are slower explosive reactions with slow shock waves and high-temperature fires. The heat may be so intense near the explosion site that it can bend or even melt steel.

- **Detonations** are faster explosions in which fires can be less intense, but the pressure and speed of the shock wave are much greater. Some shock waves may move at 9 kilometres (6 miles) per second. They can shatter or bend objects and structures in their way and propel pieces of debris incredibly fast and far.

Blast investigation

Fire investigators often start by looking at the remains of materials affected by a blast. They can learn a lot from these! When metal structures have melted, this might indicate a deflagration. If metal structures are bent or shattered, a detonation is the more likely culprit.

A forensic investigator in a laboratory uses an electronic smelling device to detect chemicals in charred debris collected at the scene of a fire.

Investigators also take samples of exploded material from different parts of a blast site back to the laboratory for close examination. When they look at a surface under a microscope, a mottled appearance or tiny pits suggests a blast of hot gas has passed over it.

In the Savenner accident, fire investigators can tell that the explosion happened inside the turpentine tanks, because each tank has a jagged hole at the top, with the metal edges bent outwards. The heat had been very intense, but there was not significant blast damage away from the tanks. The turpentine inside exploded in a deflagration.

Vapour danger

Most explosive reactions need high temperatures or an electrical spark to start. In the Savenner accident, investigators look at diagrams and records of how the turpentine had been stored. They suspect that the fire may have resulted from a build-up of vapour that turned to fire.

Vapour is another word for the gas form of a substance. It can also mean tiny droplets of it suspended in air. Turpentine evaporates at a low temperature, and it is the vapour that burns, rather than the liquid. The vapour can set on fire at the sort of temperatures you might expect on a very hot day.

Petrol is flammable and evaporates easily at low temperatures. like turpentine. At petrol stations. people should never light flames or even use cell phones. which could create an electrical spark. This might ignite petrol vapour.

If it is warm outside, it would be even hotter inside a metal tank. That is why the Savenner tanks had pipes removing the vapour to a separate, small drum for storage. These drums were filled with pieces of special **charcoal** that has lots of holes, like a sponge, giving it a large surface area. These pieces of charcoal acted as **filters**. Substances like turpentine attach to the charcoal surfaces, are trapped, and then cannot react.

YOU'RE THE INVESTIGATOR!

Why did the turpentine ignite if it was sealed in a tank and its vapours were controlled by charcoal drums? As an investigator, you need to find out. (See page 24 for the answer.)

Gases and reactions

Molecules of a substance are more spaced out and move faster in a gas than in a liquid. Substances such as fuels usually burn more easily as a vapour than as a liquid. This is because each molecule of the substance is more spaced out and therefore is surrounded by more oxygen molecules. (Remember, one of the three things that fire needs is oxygen!) Even solids can burn and explode more easily when they are in tiny rather than large pieces. This is because they have a larger surface area for the reaction to start. For example, in coal mines, people have to be very careful not to create sparks, as these could start a dangerous reaction because of the coal dust in the air.

In liquid form. turpentine molecules are in close contact with each other. As a vapour. turpentine molecules may be surrounded by oxygen molecules they can react with. especially at higher temperatures.

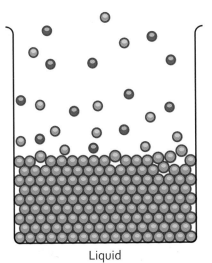

Liquid

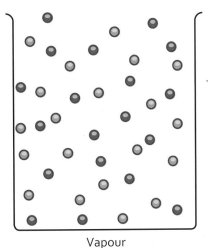

Vapour

⬤ - Turpentine molecule

⬤ - Oxygen molecule

In the drums

The fire investigators' next job is to check how the vapour storage drum had been set up. Chemical industries, like all others, should have safety equipment and procedures in place to help prevent accidents. Investigators need to know what went wrong here.

The investigators discover from maintenance records that the carbon in the drum had not been cleaned for several weeks. This matters for two reasons. First, the spaces in the charcoal had gradually filled up, so the filter was removing less vapour. Second, heat is given out as charcoal traps the turpentine molecules. The hot charcoal would have warmed the growing number of unattached turpentine molecules when the filter became full.

Charcoal is a useful filter for removing all kinds of odours and hazardous substances from the air. For example, it can keep trainers smelling sweet!

The inspectors also discover that the drums were missing some important equipment, which could have prevented the heat in the carbon from starting a fire. There was a pipe from the drum that allowed a small amount of excess vapour to be released into the atmosphere. This should have had a one-way valve on it – to stop air from flowing back into the drum – but it had a two-way valve (meaning gases could flow in both directions). If it had been a one-way valve, there would have been no oxygen for the turpentine in the drum to react with.

They also find that the pipe leading between the drum and the turpentine tanks had no **flame arrestor** fitted. This is a special device that forces any flame through very narrow channels, where it can no longer burn.

YOU'RE THE INVESTIGATOR!: THE ANSWER

Why did the fire begin in the carbon drum and move through pipes into the turpentine tanks? It was because important safety features were missing.

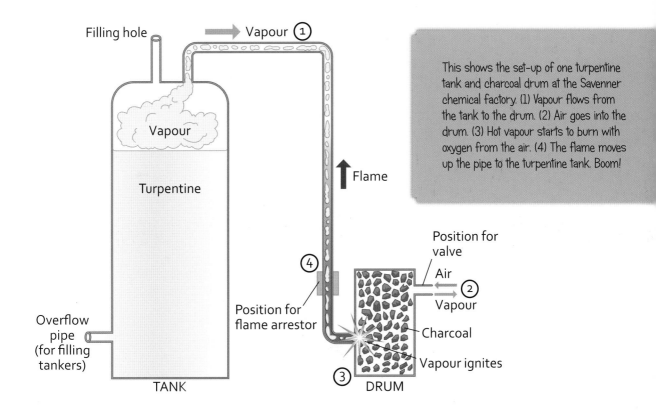

Filling hole → Vapour ①

Vapour

Turpentine

Overflow pipe (for filling tankers)

TANK

Flame

④ Position for flame arrestor

Position for valve

Air

Vapour ②

Charcoal

Vapour ignites

③ DRUM

This shows the set-up of one turpentine tank and charcoal drum at the Savenner chemical factory. (1) Vapour flows from the tank to the drum. (2) Air goes into the drum. (3) Hot vapour starts to burn with oxygen from the air. (4) The flame moves up the pipe to the turpentine tank. Boom!

The investigators' main hypothesis about how the fire started is:

Vapours move from the tank to the drum.

↓

Uncleaned charcoal gets hot in the drum.

↓

Air moves into the drum.

↓

Oxygen in the air reacts with fuel, starting a fire.

↓

A flame arrestor is missing, so fire burns inside the pipe connecting the drum to the tanks.

↓

Turpentine vapours in the tanks explode, causing the tanks to rupture.

↓

Turpentine spills out and ignites.

EVIDENCE REPORT

Vapour control drum specifications:

Volume: 225 litres (50 gallons)
Contents: Activated charcoal
Surface area of charcoal: 1,500 square metres per gram
Flame arrestor: No
Type of valve to atmosphere: Two-way
Target chemical: Turpentine
Flash point (temperature when vapour starts to burn):
    32–46 degrees Celsius
    (90–115 degrees Fahrenheit)
Lower explosive limit: less than 1 per cent turpentine in air

Dangerous gas

Raging fire and black smoke came from burning turpentine and buildings at the Savenner chemical factory. This was a major hazard in itself. But the morning after the fire, there is a new hazard. A cloud of gas spreads from the accident site, and soon there are reports of people coughing, choking, and having watering eyes. What is going on?

In store

Accident investigators look at records of what substances were being made and also stored at the factory, in addition to the turpentine. There were three liquids in three separate tanks. Hydrochloric **acid** was stored in one tank for use in the factory and for use elsewhere as an industrial cleaner. Sodium hydrosulfide was in another tank, and it was used to process paper and leather. The third tank contained a fire retardant, meaning a liquid that could be used to make foam to help put out fires. However, there were no gases stored in any tanks, and none of the liquids would turn into a vapour easily. Investigators realize that the gas released by the incident must be the product of a chemical reaction.

Health concerns

Health workers help those injured at the accident site and beyond. They can also help investigators work out what sorts of chemical hazards have been produced or released by the accident. Health-care workers are among the first people at an accident site. They examine patients' symptoms so they can treat injuries and organize getting victims to the hospital for additional medical care.

People's symptoms can be important clues for the investigative team. For example, people poisoned with cyanide develop an unusual bright pink or reddish colour to their skin. In the case of the Savenner accident, the symptoms are severe eye irritation and breathing difficulties. This could have been caused by quite a few different gases – although there is an unpleasant smell of rotten eggs in the area.

YOU'RE THE INVESTIGATOR!

Eyewitnesses a couple of hundred metres away from the accident site reported that they could smell rotten eggs early in the morning after the explosion. Why couldn't the people living close smell anything? (See page 30 for the answer.)

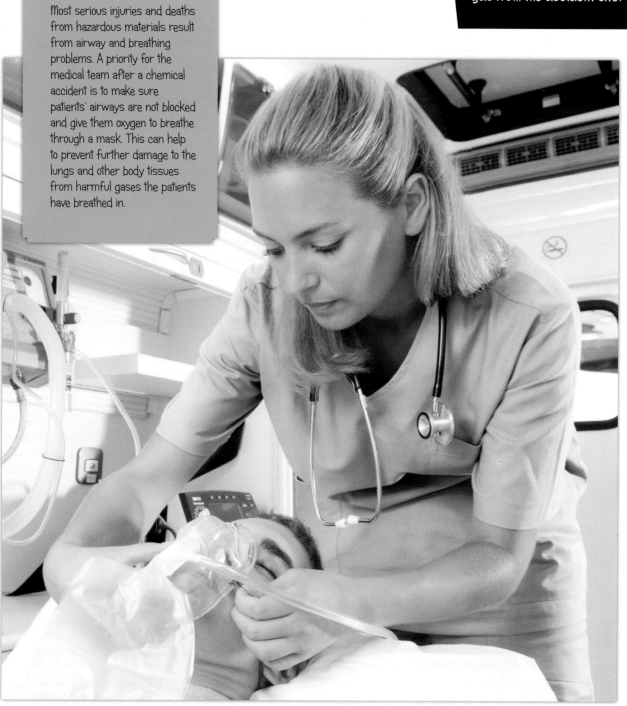

Most serious injuries and deaths from hazardous materials result from airway and breathing problems. A priority for the medical team after a chemical accident is to make sure patients' airways are not blocked and give them oxygen to breathe through a mask. This can help to prevent further damage to the lungs and other body tissues from harmful gases the patients have breathed in.

Day 2, 7.00 a.m.
People start to show symptoms of exposure to gas from the accident site.

Testing the air

The smell in the air suggests to investigators that the gas causing the injuries is hydrogen sulfide. However, they need more evidence to confirm this, because large quantities of hydrogen sulfide can affect a person's ability to smell!

EVIDENCE REPORT

The following shows what levels of hydrogen sulfide are dangerous, and what health problems they cause:

Danger	Concentration (milligrams of hydrogen sulfide in every litre of air)	Health impact
Low	0.005	People can smell a rotten egg odour
	10–20	Eye irritation
	50–100	Possible eye damage
	100–150	Nerves in nose paralysed, so the person cannot smell the gas
	320–530	Lung damage that can be potentially lethal
	800	Lethal after five minutes breathing in the gas
Highest	1,000	Immediate collapse and breathing failure

Investigators urgently need to identify the gas, in order to work out how dangerous it could be and how far it could spread. So, they use special monitoring equipment to check the types and levels of substances in the air at the site. Some of this equipment has electrochemical **sensors** inside. These are like batteries that create a particular current, or flow, of electric charge when exposed to a particular gas. The device can distinguish between different gases by the currents they produce. Several tests confirm the investigators' suspicions and fears: the gas in the air is hydrogen sulfide.

An accident investigator uses a device to measure air quality following a gas well fire in Chengdu, China.

Escaping the gas

Hydrogen sulfide is a poison. It can be **lethal** in large quantities, and in smaller amounts it can also cause temporary or permanent eye and lung problems. The investigators have no choice but to quickly **evacuate** residents living near the factory. This is where levels of hydrogen sulfide are greatest.

Day 2, 8.15 a.m.
The gas is confirmed as being hydrogen sulfide.

9.00 a.m.
An evacuation begins.

Hazmat suits are worn by people dealing with accident scenes if they are at risk of being exposed to hazardous materials. The suits cover their whole bodies including their breathing apparatus, and are made of materials resistant to damage.

Evacuees are also warned about how to leave safely. The local authorities are not able to give out gas masks quickly, so they instruct people to cover their mouths with a cloth, to avoid breathing in the dangerous gas. In other chemical accidents, people are warned not to touch or walk into mists of gas, spilled liquids, and other possible hazards. The evacuees remain in a shelter, where they will be cared for until **concentrations** (levels) of the gas have fallen.

Acids and alkalis

How did hydrogen sulfide get into the air? Fire investigators discover that the heat of the fire had melted plastic pipes coming out of the tanks. This meant that substances could spill out, mix, and react together. The two most likely substances to react were hydrochloric acid and sodium hydrosulfide, which is an **alkali**.

Acids and alkalis are different sorts of substances. You may have tested the **pH** of acids and alkalis using litmus paper or solution and seen that they produce different colours. Weak acids, such as lemon juice, are sour to taste. Strong acids, such as hydrochloric acid, can break down materials such as metals and react with many substances. They are also very dangerous because they easily damage human tissue. Weak alkalis are often soapy to the touch, but strong ones such as sodium hydroxide or sodium hydrosulfide can be as dangerous as strong acids. Never test an acid or alkali by touching or tasting it.

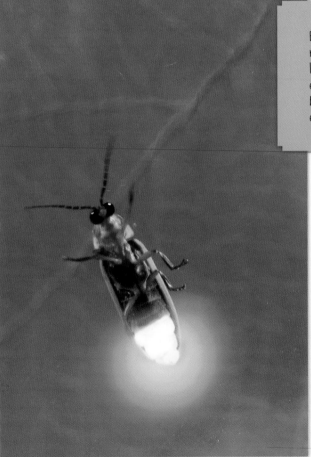

Energy released during a reaction can also create light. Fireflies use light from exothermic reactions in their bodies to communicate with each other.

YOU'RE THE INVESTIGATOR!: THE ANSWER

The concentration of hydrogen sulfide was higher closer to the accident site. People closest to it could not smell it because high concentrations were affecting their ability to smell.

The reaction

One definition of an alkali is that it reacts with an acid, producing a substance that is called a salt. In the reaction, the alkali **neutralizes** the acid, because the pH gets closer to neutral. Most neutralization reactions also produce water. For example:

sodium hydroxide + hydrochloric acid ➝ sodium chloride + water
$NaOH + HCl$ ➝ $NaCl + H_2O$

Other acids and alkali neutralization reactions produce a salt and a gas.
This is what happened in the accident:

sodium hydrosulfide + hydrochloric acid ➝ sodium chloride + hydrogen sulfide
$NaHS + HCl$ ➝ $NaCl + H_2S$

Firefighters stopped the reaction by spraying lots of water and foam on the reactants. This cooled the reactants, so there was less energy to continue reacting. It also gradually diluted them. This means that the molecules of each reactant were spaced further apart, and were then less likely to meet and react.

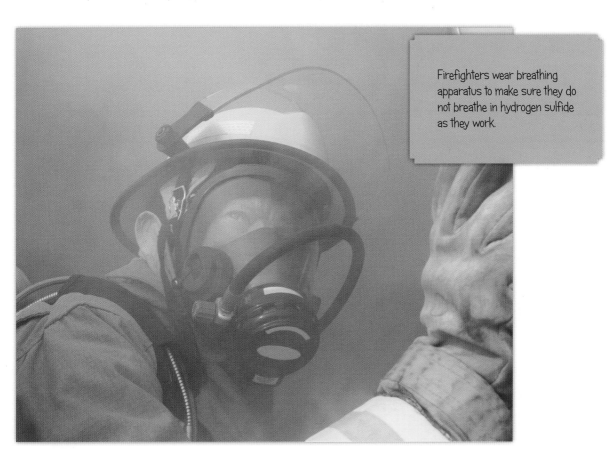

Firefighters wear breathing apparatus to make sure they do not breathe in hydrogen sulfide as they work.

Elements, the periodic table, and reactivity

An element is a substance made of one type of atom. For example, pure gold and oxygen are elements. The periodic table shows all the elements as chemical symbols. The way they are arranged is not random. Metals such as sodium (Na) are on the left, and non-metals such as sulfur (S) and chlorine (Cl) are on the right. Elements with similar properties are put together in columns called groups. One important property is **reactivity**.

You may know about the reactivity series of metals. This is a listing of them by most and least reactive when heated or added to water. Potassium and sodium are the most reactive in this group, and platinum and gold are the least reactive. Reactivity is a chemical property of a substance. It shows how easily its atoms gain or lose the electrons used for bonding with other atoms.

More reactive ↓

		More reactive ↓			Less reactive ↓			More reactive ↓									
hydrogen H																	helium He
lithium Li	beryllium Be										boron B	carbon C	nitrogen N	oxygen O	fluorine F	neon Ne	
sodium Na	magnesium Mg										aluminium Al	silicon Si	phosphorus P	sulfur S	chlorine Cl	argon Ar	
potassium K	calcium Ca	scandium Sc	titanium Ti	vanadium V	chromium Cr	manganese Mn	iron Fe	cobalt Co	nickel Ni	copper Cu	zinc Zn	gallium Ga	germanium Ge	arsenic As	selenium Se	bromine Br	krypton Kr
rubidium Rb	strontium Sr	yttrium Y	zirconium Zr	niobium Nb	molybdenum Mo	technetium Tc	ruthenium Ru	rhodium Rh	palladium Pd	silver Ag	cadmium Cd	indium In	tin Sn	antimony Sb	tellurium Te	iodine I	xenon Xe
caesium Cs	barium Ba		hafnium Hf	tantalum Ta	tungsten W	rhenium Re	osmium Os	iridium Ir	platinum Pt	gold Au	mercury Hg	thallium Tl	lead Pb	bismuth Bi	polonium Po	astatine At	radon Rn
francium Fr	radium Ra																

More reactive ↓ (top right, pointing to He)

Least reactive ↑ (bottom right, pointing to Rn)

More reactive ↑ (bottom left, pointing to Fr)

Chemists can use the periodic table to predict whether a reaction will occur. For example, sodium is more reactive than chlorine, but it is less reactive than hydrogen. So, scientists could predict that the hydrogen from hydrogen chloride would bond with the sodium from sodium hydrosulfide – in preference to the chlorine – and form hydrogen sulfide.

ANALYTICAL CHEMIST

Analytical chemists investigate substances to understand how they behave and react in different conditions.

The job involves analysing samples of substances using scientific methods such as spectroscopy (measuring how atoms absorb and emit light differently). Some chemists work in preventing the **contamination** of medicines by other, unwanted substances. Most analytical chemists have a degree in chemistry or biochemistry as well as experience working in scientific laboratories.

Knowing your substances

In the Savenner accident, the release of hydrogen sulfide was the result of two substances combining. There might not have been a reaction if those substances had been stored further apart. All substances should be clearly labelled, so that people know what they are and know their reactivity. Labelling helps workers in factories know how best to store different substances, and it warns emergency workers of the dangers of accidentally spilled or released substances.

Hazardous materials are labelled using a familiar classification system to show their reactivity danger. For example, class 1 hazards are explosives, and class 2 hazards include flammable gases. Any person can see that this tank contains toxic chemicals that would be harmful to fish if released into the sea.

Environmental impact

Accident investigators have discovered what caused the explosion at the Savenner chemical factory: fire and the release of poisonous gas. But they have another mystery to solve. In the river near the factory, fish are dying.

So, team members with special knowledge of environmental conditions get to work. They assess how substances released during the accident have spread in the surrounding area. They collect data on weather and other environmental conditions, to see if these had any impact on the accident. They also work to find the best and safest ways to clear up the **pollution**.

Temperature effects

Changes in air temperature can cause changes in stored substances. Records supplied by meteorologists (see the box) show that the temperature was very hot during the day, but it was unusually cold on the night before the explosion.

YOU'RE THE INVESTIGATOR!

Turpentine was found in the nearby river, yet it was separated by 500 metres (a third of a mile) of dry land. The tanks were in a concrete-walled enclosure, and there was no rain to wash turpentine in. How did it get there? (Find the answer on page 37.)

High external temperatures increase the evaporation of some substances. They also make some gases and liquids expand, because their molecules move faster. This puts extra stress on the tanks and valves used to contain them.

PBC-4
V·5000м³

ОГНЕОПАСНО

Day 3, 7.00 a.m.
Fishermen notice dead fish
in the river.

METEOROLOGIST

Meteorologists study present and past trends and patterns in the atmosphere, weather, and climate (long-term patterns of weather throughout the year).

Some meteorologists specialize in forecasting weather in the future, which could have an impact, for example, on farmers, water suppliers, and outdoor event organizers. Others develop and use equipment to collect wind, cloud, rain, and air pressure data. Meteorologists need good computer skills to analyse complex weather data, and many have a degree in maths or physics.

During the chilly night, the warm turpentine vapour in the main tank, pipes, and charcoal drum would have cooled. Some may have condensed back into liquid turpentine. But the remaining cooling vapour would have taken up less space, lowering the pressure in the tank. The greater pressure outside would have pushed air from outside into the charcoal drum. This would explain what started the fire. When oxygen moved over hot vapour, it started the burning reaction.

When an accident happens investigators need to know the temperature and other atmospheric conditions. This is not only to see if they contributed to the accident happening, but also how they may affect the spread of the accident in the coming days and weeks.

Moving around

Substances released in an accident spread out in different ways. For example, high wind speeds can blow the substances long distances, but also disperse them so they are less concentrated. Low winds and **humid** air can trap and concentrate airborne substances near ground level around the accident site. This is what happened to the hydrogen sulfide gas in Savenner for several days.

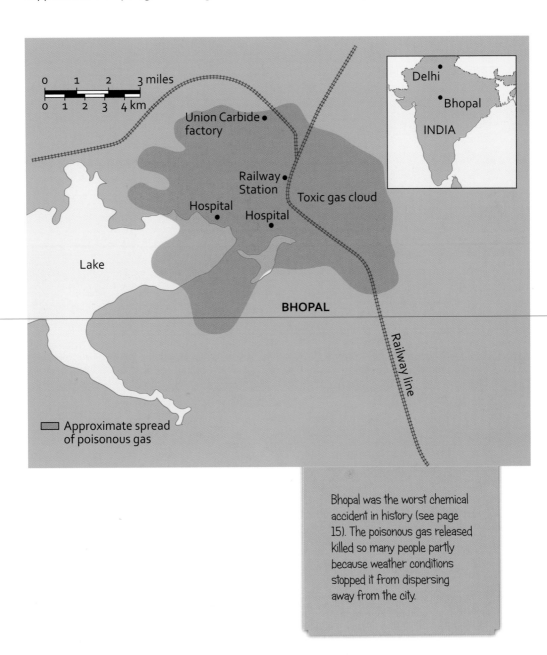

Bhopal was the worst chemical accident in history (see page 15). The poisonous gas released killed so many people partly because weather conditions stopped it from dispersing away from the city.

Substances spilled on land may soak into soil or wash into water. In rivers and seas, waves and currents spread substances. In water, substances may float, sink, or dissolve or react with the water. For example, turpentine molecules are less dense than water molecules, so they float. Turpentine is also insoluble in water (meaning it does not dissolve), and it is unreactive with water.

Scientists predict how **pollutants** will disperse (spread out) using computer models. These are programs that show how changing weather would affect how pollutants move around. The models use data on wind direction, temperature, and humidity, as well as data on the size and properties of the particular substance that has been released.

Gas to water

Some gases released into the atmosphere can react to form other harmful substances. For example, hydrogen sulfide can react with oxygen in the air, forming sulfur oxides. These react with water vapour in the atmosphere, forming dilute sulfuric acid.

The acids fall to earth as something called acid rain, which has a lower pH than normal rain. The acidity can damage the leaves of trees and prevent their roots from taking in nutrients from the soil. Raising the acidity in lakes can also damage living things, such as snails that cannot grow shells properly. Acid rain reacts with some types of stone and can speed up the erosion (wearing away) of buildings.

YOU'RE THE INVESTIGATOR!: THE ANSWER

How did the turpentine end up in the river? Water sprayed onto the fire by firefighters spilled out of the enclosure with the tanks in it because the wall cracked in the heat. This washed turpentine into the river.

The river

Dead fish and the strong, distinctive smell are the obvious signs that turpentine got into the nearby river after the accident. Turpentine has several effects on living things. It can coat the skin of frogs and the gills of fish, preventing them from taking in sufficient oxygen for respiration. (Respiration is an essential life process by which oxygen is used to release energy from food.) When aquatic animals accidentally eat turpentine, it can also damage their internal organs, such as the liver or stomach.

At the Savenner accident, freshwater biologists continue the investigation. They collect water samples to see whether there are any other chemical effects from the accident. There is no change in the acidity of the water compared with records of water quality in the past. This proves that the hydrogen sulfide released in the accident has not reacted with water to form sulfuric acid.

FRESHWATER BIOLOGIST

Freshwater biologists study the living things in lakes, streams, and rivers.

The work of a freshwater biologist involves sampling and identifying organisms living in water, such as snails, worms, and plankton. They study environmental conditions, the ways organisms interact with their environment and each other, and the impact of human activity on freshwater all around the world. Freshwater biologists will have generally studied biology at university.

Chemical spills can wash into and pollute drinking water supplies that human populations rely on.

Biological clues

Biologists can learn a lot by studying populations of living things in rivers and lakes. Animals and plants breed, grow, and thrive best in particular environmental conditions. A healthy, unpolluted river will have a rich variety of **organisms** that interact with each other. For example, tiny, plant-like organisms that are part of **plankton** produce their own food by a process called photosynthesis. Small fish eat the plankton, and pike eat the small fish.

A chemical spill can kill organisms that are sensitive to pollution, and this may affect other animals. For example, when a small fish eats many plankton over time, each with some turpentine in them, the amount of turpentine in the fish can build up to poisonous levels. Also, if turpentine kills too many small fish, populations of larger fish may shrink because they have less food.

Day 3,
9.00 a.m.–10.00a.m.
Freshwater biologists confirm there is turpentine in the river.

The darter is an important indicator species used to assess the health of North American rivers.

Living things that are sensitive to environmental change are called **indicator species**. They are often the first sign of a problem in an ecosystem (community of organisms), and so biologists monitor indicator species populations closely. Some important indicator species in rivers include fish, frogs, and invertebrates (animals without backbones or internal skeletons) such as leeches.

Clean-up

To limit the environmental damage caused by a chemical accident, it is important to clear the spilled or released substances as soon as possible. In the Savenner accident, experts remove the turpentine from the river by soaking it up in materials such as sponges and cloth, which they then dispose of in bags that are burned in special furnaces. When soil is contaminated, people may use backhoes to excavate soil, which is then put into secure landfill sites where it cannot harm people, react, or pollute water sources.

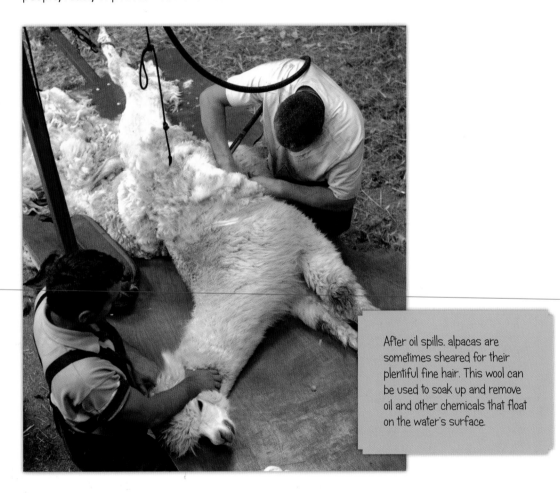

After oil spills, alpacas are sometimes sheared for their plentiful fine hair. This wool can be used to soak up and remove oil and other chemicals that float on the water's surface.

Chemical accidents can also be cleaned up using chemical reactions. Experts sometimes use oxidizing reactions. This means they combine atoms in the pollutant with oxygen. This makes less harmful products, such as water and carbon dioxide. For example, people dig a well, and pump solutions containing hydrogen peroxide and potassium permanganate into the contaminated soil around it. Sometimes they add iron as a catalyst (a substance that speeds up a reaction), to help the hydrogen peroxide work more quickly.

Other problems following chemical accidents can be cleaned up using neutralization reactions. For example, planes may dump calcium carbonate powder onto lakes where the water has become too acidic with sulfuric acid. The calcium carbonate reacts with the acid to produce calcium sulfate (a salt), water, and carbon dioxide. These substances make the water less acidic.

Cleaning with micro-organisms

Some spills of substances, such as oil and pesticides (chemicals that kill or deter organisms from eating or damaging crops), may be cleaned up using **micro-organisms** such as bacteria and protozoa. Some of these micro-organisms feed on certain harmful substances in the pollutants. The micro-organisms may already live in soil and groundwater that have been contaminated, but others are grown artificially and sprayed onto places that need particular substances to be removed. People may pump in oxygen or add nutrients, including molasses, to help the micro-organisms grow and work faster in these places. Using living things to clear up pollution is called bioremediation.

Two boats drag a boom towards an oil spill. This both absorbs and contains the oil in one area, where it can be removed.

End of the investigation

The team of investigators has completed the first part of their work. They have thought of hypotheses about why the accident may have happened. For example, the fire started in the charcoal drums, and then a reaction occurred to release hydrogen sulfide gas. They have assembled a wide range of data. These include eyewitness reports, weather data, and documents confirming missing safety equipment.

Causes

The investigators' next step is to put together a report showing how the data supports their hypotheses. They make conclusions about the different causes of the accident.

- *Direct causes*: Direct causes are major conditions or events that made an accident happen. For example, kicking a football at a window is a direct cause for the window breaking. In the case of the Savenner chemical accident, a direct cause is acid and alkali reacting. Another direct cause is heat damaging the wall, allowing turpentine to escape from the enclosure.

- *Contributing causes*: Taken together, contributing causes increase the likelihood of an accident happening, for example, using a hard leather football rather than a soft one if it is kicked near a window. For the chemical accident, these include a missing flame arrestor and dirty charcoal in the tank that was supposed to remove turpentine vapour.

Poor maintenance of equipment was the root cause of an accident at the Texas City refinery in 2005. Workers filled a tall tower with jet fuel, but safety valves were not working, so the fuel spilled out. A spark from a car with its engine running accidentally ignited the vapour. The blast and fire injured 170 workers and killed 15.

- *Root causes*: Root causes are the underlying reasons that, if corrected, could prevent another accident, such as never playing football near windows! The root causes of the chemical accident were that the substances that could react dangerously were stored too close together, and that the vapour control system for the storage tanks was inadequate.

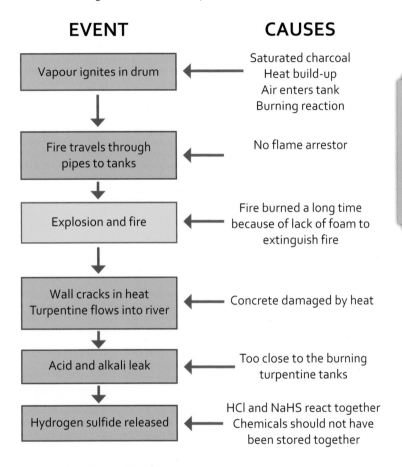

EVENT   CAUSES

EVENT	CAUSES
Vapour ignites in drum	Saturated charcoal Heat build-up Air enters tank Burning reaction
Fire travels through pipes to tanks	No flame arrestor
Explosion and fire	Fire burned a long time because of lack of foam to extinguish fire
Wall cracks in heat Turpentine flows into river	Concrete damaged by heat
Acid and alkali leak	Too close to the burning turpentine tanks
Hydrogen sulfide released	HCl and NaHS react together Chemicals should not have been stored together

Investigators make a flow chart to sum up the sequence of events and causes of the Savenner chemical factory accident.

CHEMICAL ENGINEER

Chemical engineers solve problems in the production and use of substances.

Some chemical engineers design, invent, and help construct chemical factories. They focus on controlling key chemical reactions, in order to safely produce substances. Others monitor factories to spot any problems that might lead to accidents or any procedures that could harm workers or the environment. Chemical engineers will have studied chemistry or engineering at university.

Mistakes in the workplace

Some estimates claim that around 9 out of 10 industrial accidents are caused by mistakes. Some are the result of working conditions. Workers are more likely to make mistakes if, for example, they do not have enough breaks during work shifts. Mistakes are also more likely when people work in places that are poorly lit or where safety equipment is inadequate.

Safe working conditions such as night shifts that are not too long can help lower the risk of chemical accidents.

In the Savenner accident, factory inspectors conclude that no individual made a mistake leading to the accident. However, they find that factory owners are partly at fault. This is because the vapour removal system was inadequate at the time of the accident. Some mistakes like this result from cutting costs. Factory owners can make more money if they spend less on safety features and hire fewer workers.

After the event

Three days after the explosion, firefighters stop the reactions causing the turpentine fire and the release of hydrogen sulfide. By five days after the event, people can return to their homes and school. Investigators by then confirm that hydrogen sulfide concentrations in air samples are low enough to be safe. The clean-up of the accident site and the polluted river are underway.

Many health and environmental impacts after an accident are very serious but short-term. These are acute impacts. For example, explosions or burns can cause horrific injuries but are not a risk once a fire is put out and possible reactants are made safe. Of course, they can have long-term health impacts. For example, people who breathe in or swallow strong acids or alkalis can develop immediate throat, lung, or stomach damage that needs long-term care. In many cases, investigators can see a clear link between the accident and the health impacts.

Some chemical accidents cause harm for long periods of time. These are called chronic impacts. For example, some hazardous substances released following accidents can remain in the environment and people living there may face continual exposure to them. The substances can have long-term effects or can gradually build up in people until they reach dangerous levels. People can then develop illnesses years later (see box below). Sometimes investigators may need to work with doctors long after an event seeking to establish a link between illnesses or medical conditions and exposure to substances in past accidents.

Day 3, 12.00 p.m.
Air monitoring reveals that the hydrogen sulfide levels are lowering.

Day 3, 6.00 p.m.
The fire is extinguished, and the reaction producing hydrogen sulfide has been stopped.

Day 5, 10.00 a.m.
Hydrogen sulfide is down to safe levels, and the evacuation is over.

Health time bomb

In 1976, a chemical accident in Meda, Italy, released a toxic cloud containing harmful substances called dioxins over the nearby city of Seveso. There were few short-term health problems, but in 2002 (26 years later), a survey discovered that women with breast cancer in Seveso had 10 times the normal amount of dioxin in their blood.

Changes

What changes are made after an industrial accident? In Savenner, the damaged area of the factory is repaired, following recommendations from investigators that it should be safer. Factory owners work with chemical engineers to design a safer chemical storage area. For example, storage tanks are fitted with working vapour control systems, spaced further apart, and kept in an enclosure built from materials that will not be damaged by fire. Heat sensors, flame arrestors, and automatic foam sprinklers are fitted to stop fires from developing. These changes will help prevent future unwanted reactions and pollution.

Small accidents may encourage individual or regional factories to make changes. Big accidents can make countries – or even the whole chemical industry – change laws and practices about safety. For example, the tragedy in Bhopal caused changes to the chemical industry in the United States (see the box on page 51).

Be prepared

People should learn lessons from accidents, but obviously it is better to improve safety before an accident happens. Engineers carry out "What if?" analyses of factories. In these, they test systems to imagine what might occur if reaction conditions change, such as a power failure affecting electrical equipment or the wrong concentration of a substance being used.

Engineers use their knowledge of the conditions in which reactions occur to anticipate any potential problems.

For example: What if there is contamination in a tank? To answer this, they find out how easy it might be for one substance to contaminate another in a factory due to mistakes, poor equipment design or positioning, electrical failure, or other problems. They test if any possible reactions are dangerous, and how many people they could endanger. They then make changes that will ensure less damage and keep people safer if a contamination does happen.

Emergency practice

Emergency response teams sometimes practise dealing with chemical accidents by pretending they are happening. For example, they check the response time when tackling fires, helping injured people, and evacuating local residents. They test how easily and rapidly emergency vehicles can get to and from the site, and how fast they can put out fires and help people who are injured.

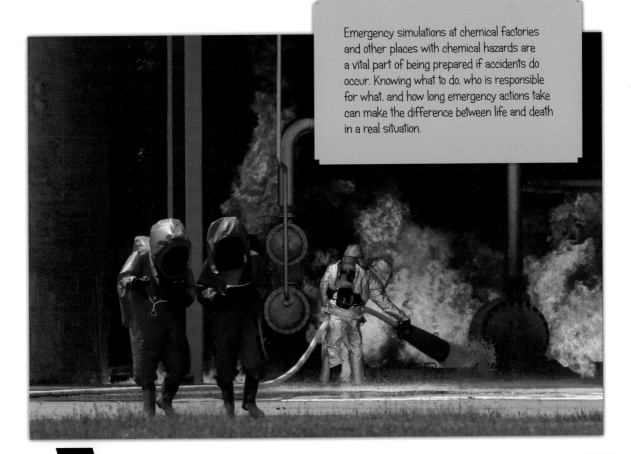

Emergency simulations at chemical factories and other places with chemical hazards are a vital part of being prepared if accidents do occur. Knowing what to do, who is responsible for what, and how long emergency actions take can make the difference between life and death in a real situation.

Investigation: a chemical reaction

For a chemical reaction to occur, the reactants must come into contact with each other. This is more likely when the reactants are in small pieces rather than in a large piece. That way, the products will be formed more quickly.

How do you think temperature would affect the speed of a reaction? Here is an investigation you can carry out. Ask an adult to help you.

Hypothesis: Chemical reactions happen faster in higher temperatures because heat energy makes different molecules move faster, and they are therefore more likely to meet and react together.

What you will need

- 4 clear cups (standard 8 ounce, or 230 millilitre, size)
- a measuring cup (for liquids)
- a thermometer (with a range of -10–110 degrees Celsius, or 0–220 degrees Fahrenheit)
- bicarbonate of soda
- citric acid powder
- a stopwatch
- a teaspoon
- notepaper
- graph paper

ABOUT THE INGREDIENTS

Bicarbonate of soda is a very weak alkali commonly used to make cakes and breads rise, and it is sold in supermarkets and health food shops. Citric acid is a weakly acidic substance found in foods such as lemons, and it is sold as a white powder in chemists and supermarkets. These ingredients are normally harmless. During the experiment, if you accidentally get either or both powders in your eyes or mouth, calmly wash it out using lots of cold tap water.

An egg fries faster in a hotter pan. The speed of chemical reaction is greater at a higher temperature.

WHAT TO DO

1. Place 4 teaspoons of bicarbonate of soda and 4 teaspoons of citric acid powder into one DRY clear cup. Mix together.

2. Measure out 100 millilitres of tap water in the measuring cup and pour it into another clear cup. Place it in a refrigerator for two hours or in a freezer until cold but not frozen. Place it on a tray or a surface that will not be damaged if you spill anything during the experiment.

3. Measure out the same volume of normal cold tap water in another clear cup and the same volume of very hot water from a tap in another cup. (BE VERY CAREFUL WHEN POURING OR CARRYING HOT WATER, SO THAT YOU DO NOT HARM YOURSELF.) Place these cups near the one containing the very cold water.

4. Use the thermometer to take the temperature of the water in each of the three cups and record it on a sheet of paper.

5. Get ready to start the stopwatch. Take one level teaspoon of the bicarbonate of soda and citric acid mix, empty it into the first cup, and start timing immediately. It will start to bubble fast, so stand back to make sure it does not splash you. Record on the paper how long it takes for the bubbling of the reaction to stop.

Very cold water

Water at room temperature

Hot water

The level of water should be the same in each cup, and the temperature recorded carefully. When you have noted the temperatures, you can start adding the powder mix to the water.

6. Repeat for the second and third cups.

7. Make a graph with the time to stop bubbling on the vertical axis and water temperature on the horizontal axis. Plot the three data points you have recorded on the graph. Draw a line between the points.

Was the reaction faster in hot compared to cold water? Does this prove your hypothesis? How would your data be affected if your teaspoons of powder were not exactly the same volume? Why?

Timeline

The investigation into the chemical accident examined throughout this book included many steps and involved many people. The course of events depended on how the accident unfolded and how long it took to carry out investigative work. Here is a timeline of what happened:

Day 1

11.00 p.m. The turpentine tanks explode at the Savenner chemical factory, starting a fire. Eyewitnesses notify authorities that there has been a possible chemical accident and call the fire department.

11.30 p.m. The fire is already out of control by the time local firefighters arrive.

Day 2

12.15 a.m. A second team of firefighters arrives to tackle the massive blaze, and they work through the night trying to prevent the flames from spreading.

6.30–7.00 a.m. A reaction between acid and alkali starts, and local people start to show symptoms of exposure to gas released from the factory.

7.15 a.m. The first people affected arrive by ambulance at the local hospital.

8.15 a.m. Investigators confirm that the gas is hydrogen sulfide. They assess how much might be produced by the volumes of substances stored at the factory. They also check weather conditions, to see how the gas might spread. Using this information, they recommend to police that they order a local evacuation and close the local school.

9.00 a.m. An evacuation begins.

12.00 p.m. Firefighters struggle to keep the blaze under control as daytime heat is at its peak.

4.00 p.m. Fire crews notice that the heat has cracked the concrete wall around the chemical storage area.

Day 3

7.00 a.m.	Fishermen notice dead fish in the river.
9.00–10.00 a.m.	Freshwater biologists confirm that there is turpentine in the river, and that this is likely to have harmed the fish.
12.00 p.m.	The fire is almost under control. Air monitoring reveals that hydrogen sulfide levels are lower at points around the factory than they were the day before.
6.00 p.m.	The fire is extinguished, and the reaction producing hydrogen sulfide has been stopped. Site inspectors move in to assess the damage and find the source of the fire.

Day 5

| 10.00 a.m. | Gas levels in the air are within safe levels, and the inspection team tells people that the evacuation is over. People start to return to their homes. Clean-up of the river begins and the school is reopened. |

The impact of chemical accidents on laws

The Bhopal chemical accident (see page 15) caused the United States to change its laws. According to these new laws, companies must inform others about hazardous substances they were using, making, and storing, and they must also make preparations for any possible accidents.

In the UK, an earlier disaster had a similar effect. In June 1974, there was an explosion at a chemical plant near Flixborough, Lincolnshire. As a result of the accident, 28 people died and 36 were seriously injured. The Flixborough disaster led to more of a focus on preventative measures. The Health and Safety Executive was set up in 1974. The Control of Industrial Major Accident Hazards (CIMAH) Regulations were established in 1984 and were replaced by the Control of Major Accident Hazards (COMAH) Regulations in 1999. These regulations are aimed at preventing or reducing the effect of major accidents on the environment and people.

Glossary

acid substance containing hydrogen with a pH value lower than 7

alkali substance that reacts with acids, making a salt and forming a solution with water with a pH greater than 7

atom smallest part of an element that can react; a building block of all matter

bond way that atoms are held together in a molecule

charcoal substance made by burning wood with a little oxygen. It is used, for example, to clean vapours from the air.

chemical change when something takes on new chemical properties

chemical reaction when a substance combines with another, making new substances

concentration measure of how many atoms or molecules of a substance are dissolved in a given volume of a mixture of substances

contamination when a substance is made dirty or dangerous because of the addition of another substance

data information, facts, or numbers collected for use or analysis

deflagration type of explosion with very hot fire but lower blast damage

detonation type of explosion with less intense fire but higher blast damage

dissolve mix with liquid and become a part of it

electron tiny piece of matter found in all atoms that has a negative charge

endothermic type of chemical reaction that takes in heat energy from its surroundings

engineering using science or maths to design, build, and use anything from structures and buildings to machines and engines

evacuate move people from somewhere dangerous – for example, because of a fire or the release of dangerous gas – to somewhere safer

evaporate when a substance physically changes from a liquid to a gas state

exothermic type of chemical reaction that gives out heat energy to its surroundings

explosion type of reaction characterized by a sudden, large, and often loud release of energy

extinguish put out – for example, to extinguish a fire by using water or another substance until it stops burning

filter device for removing pieces of solid or impurities from a liquid or gas passed through it

flame arrestor device that stops a flame from burning

flammable something that burns easily

forensic using scientific techniques to investigate possible crimes or to resolve other matters of law

hazardous risky or dangerous to an organism's health or safety

humid when air is warm and damp

hypothesis idea or explanation for something that awaits proof using scientific observation, data, and conclusions based on the data

indicator species type of organism affected by small changes in environmental conditions that can be used to represent other organisms in the same habitat

lethal capable of causing death

micro-organism type of tiny living thing, such as bacteria, that cannot easily be seen without a microscope

molecule two or more atoms grouped together

neutralize in chemistry, to raise the pH of an acid or lower the pH of an alkali. A neutralization reaction between an acid and an alkali creates a solution with a pH around 7.

nucleus tiny, central part of an atom around which electrons move

organism living thing

pH measure of the level of acidity or alkalinity in a solution

physical change change in the shape, size, or state of a substance that involves no chemical change

plankton tiny living things found in water

pollutant something that dirties or spoils an environment

pollution when harmful or unwanted substances are introduced into the environment

product in chemistry, the product is what is produced by a chemical reaction

reactant in chemistry, reactants are the substances that change during a chemical reaction

reactivity chemical property of a substance showing how ready it is to form new substances with others through chemical reactions

sensor device that can react to light, sound, heat, or another stimulus to make a machine work

shock wave movement of powerful air pressure caused by an explosion

vapour gas form of a substance, sometimes with tiny liquid droplets

Find out more

Books

Chemical Reactions (Science Essentials: Chemistry), Denise Walker (Evans, 2007)

From Gunpowder to Laser Chemistry – Discovering Chemical Reactions (Chain Reactions), Andrew Solway (Heinemann Library, 2008)

The Dynamic World of Chemical Reactions (Graphic Science), Agnieszka Biskup (Capstone, 2012)

What's Chemistry All About? (Science Stories), Alex Frith and Lisa Jane Gillespie (Usborne, 2012)

Websites

www.bbc.co.uk/bitesize/ks3/science/chemical_material_behaviour/ph_experiment/activity
This web page helps you to carry out experiments to find the PH values of different items.

www.bbc.co.uk/bitesize/standard/chemistry/elementsandreactions/chemical_reactions/revision/1
Learn about chemical reactions on this BBC website.

www.chem4kids.com/files/react_intro.html
This is a good resource for understanding chemical reactions.

www.factsonline.nl
Want to know the details of more chemical accidents? This website provides access to a database of over 24,000 chemical accidents involving hazardous substances over the last century.

www.futuremorph.org/11-13/next-steps [www.futuremorph.org/14-16]
Find out more about careers in science by looking on the Future Morph website run by the Science Council.

www.oum.ox.ac.uk/thezone/minerals/define/chemical.htm
Discover more about atoms and compounds on this site.

www.syngentaperiodictable.co.uk/periodic-table.php?keyStage=4
Discover more about the periodic table on this website.

Topics to research

- Nuclear accidents are similar to chemical accidents but involve the release of radioactive substances and radiation. Find out what radiation is, why it is a hazard to people, and the long-term effects of nuclear accidents. To help you do this, research the following major nuclear accidents: Chernobyl (Russia), Three Mile Island (USA), and Fukushima (Japan).

- Substances do not have to be released in accidents to be a hazard. Ingredients used in household products can gradually build up in the environment, causing problems. For example, disposable nappies often contain small amounts of dioxins, the same chemical that caused such problems at Seveso (see page 45). Dioxins can get into water supplies from used nappies left to rot on rubbish dumps. Find out about hidden hazards in household products and what safer alternatives are available.

- Release of harmful chemicals has been used throughout history as a weapon of war. Research the following: Agent Orange, mustard gas, sarin.

- Imagine you live near a chemical factory. Make a poster demanding less secrecy about what they make there and the hazards, better safety in the factory, and better preparedness for accidents. Use illustrations and slogans to get your message across effectively.

Index